Gangs and Self-Esteem

TOOKIE SPEAKS OUT AGAINST GANG VIOLENCE™

Stanley "Tookie" Williams

with Barbara Cottman Becnel

The Rosen Publishing Group's

PowerKids Press™
New York

Published in 1996 by The Rosen Publishing Group, Inc.
29 East 21st Street, New York, NY 10010

First Edition

Book design: Kim Sonsky

Photo credits: Cover © Barbara Ureye/International Stock; front cover inset, back cover, and p. 4 © J. Patrick Forden; p. 7 L. J. Schneider/International Stock; p. 8 © AP/Wide World Photos; p.11 © D. Copaken/Gamma Liaison; p. 12 © Rihh/Gamma Liaison; p. 15 © Bill Stanton/International Stock; p. 16 by Maria Moreno; p. 19 © Jeff Greenberg/International Stock; p. 20 © Laurie Bayer/International Stock.

Williams, Stanley.
    Gangs and self-esteem / by Stanley "Tookie" Williams and Barbara Cottman Becnel.
        p.   cm. — (Tookie speaks out against gang violence)
    Includes index.
    Summary: A co-founder of the Crips extolls the benefits of not joining a gang.
    ISBN 0-8239-2344-4
    1. Gangs—United States—Juvenile literature. 2. Self-esteem—Juvenile literature. 3. Williams, Stanley—Juvenile literature. [1. Gangs. 2. Self-esteem.] I. Becnel, Barbara Cottman. II. Title. III. Series: Williams, Stanley. Tookie speaks out against gang violence.
    HV6439.U5W56 1996
    364.1'06'60973—dc20   96-3292
                                                                    CIP
                                                                    AC

Manufactured in the United States of America

Contents

My "Rep"

Hi, I'm Tookie—that's my nickname. My real name is Stanley Williams. I grew up in South Central Los Angeles. When I was your age, I got into a lot of fights that other boys started. Then one day I decided I should throw the first punch.

By the time I was a teenager, I had a "rep" or **reputation** (rep-yoo-TAY-shun). People all over South Central talked about me being a good fighter. Even people I didn't know had heard stories about me. And they were afraid of me.

◀ *Tookie learned that having a good rep feels better than having a bad rep.*

Feeling Important

I used to like it when people talked about me. It didn't matter that they were scared of me. I liked having a rep, even a bad rep. It made me feel important.

I thought that by beating up people I was cool and tough. I thought that was the way to get people to **respect** (re-SPEKT) me, to look up to me. I thought I had good **self-esteem** (SELF-es-TEEM), that I respected myself. But I was wrong. I just didn't know any other way to feel good about myself.

It's up to you to decide whether you want to have a good rep or a bad rep. ▶

Meeting Raymond

When I met Raymond Washington, I was in high school. He came to my schoolyard to talk to me. Raymond wanted me—and all my friends—to start a gang with him. He wanted the gang to fight the other street gangs in South Central. My rep as a fighter made Raymond want me to join him. Raymond also had a rep for fighting. We started a gang called the Crips.

The Crips and the Bloods are two gangs in South Central Los Angeles.

The Crips' Rep

The Crips soon had a rep for being **violent** (VY-o-lent). Our rep spread through South Central. As more people talked about us, more kids wanted to be like us. Some kids were so afraid of us that they joined the Crips so they didn't have to fight us.

We Crips liked our rep. But to keep up our bad rep, we had to hurt people.

Many gang members think they need to hurt others for people to respect them. ▶

Gangbanging

At first, we beat up other kids. Then we began to be more violent. We started to do other bad things like sell drugs and rob people and stores. We used violence to get what we wanted. People called that **gangbanging** (GANG-bang-ing). Gang-banging makes a gang member's bad rep grow bigger and bigger. But getting a bad rep and gangbanging causes a lot of trouble and pain—for everyone.

◀ *Gangbangers risk being caught and arrested.*

13

My Big Mistake

I believed that because people were afraid of me, they respected me. That was one of my biggest mistakes. Respect cannot be earned by using violence to scare people. When people are afraid of you, they want to hurt *you* before you hurt them.

The bad rep I was so proud of didn't cause anyone to really like or respect me.

People who are afraid often feel the need to protect themselves. ▶

Bad Self-Esteem

Many gang members think they respect themselves. They think they have good self-esteem because they feel good about their bad reps. But they are wrong. So were we. There's no such thing as having good self-esteem when you're hurting other people. That is bad self-esteem, and nothing good can come from it.

Good Self-Esteem

Good self-esteem comes from respecting yourself and others. Respecting yourself means liking yourself. When you truly like yourself, you don't hurt yourself or others. When you have good self-esteem, you don't **disrespect** (DIS-re-SPEKT) yourself by doing things that will get you or others into trouble.

It took me a long time to learn to like myself. But I do now, and it feels much better than having a bad rep.

There are lots of things you can do to feel good about yourself, such as working hard in school. ▶

Having a Good Rep

Anyone can have a rep. *You* decide whether you want it to be good or bad. You can get a good rep from working hard in school, being friendly to others, being fair and honest, listening to your parents and teachers, and not joining a gang.

A bad rep—like a gangbanging rep—only hurts you and everyone else in the end.

◀ *When you have a good rep, you respect yourself and others.*

A Good Rep Feels Great

It feels great having a good rep. You feel good because you respect yourself. You have good self-esteem. But you have to work at getting a good rep. Every day you have to make smart choices about what you do.

If you already have a bad rep, it will take time to change it. But that's okay. Everybody has to work hard to have a good rep. So keep trying to be a good person. I did it. You can do it too. I know you can.

Glossary

disrespect (DIS-re-SPEKT) To think of and treat yourself or someone else poorly.

gangbanging (GANG-bang-ing) Gangs using violence against other people, sometimes to commit crimes.

reputation (rep-yoo-TAY-shun) What people say and think about you.

respect (re-SPEKT) To think highly of yourself or someone else.

self-esteem (SELF-es-TEEM) How you feel about yourself.

violent (VY-o-lent) Hurting yourself or others.

Index